New Teac

2nd Edition

*How To Get Through Your First Year of
Teaching and Maintain Your Sanity*

by Dino Mangano

TO SCHEDULE PERSONALIZED COACHING
WITH DINO,
IN PERSON OR ONLINE

www.ManganoCoaching.com

Dedicated to Margaret, my ultimate mentor teacher.

Table of Contents

Introduction

You're reading this book, that means you're a teacher. It means you saw the title, and something stood out to you. THAT means you're probably a new teacher who is stressed out. (Even if you're a veteran, don't worry, this will still be a valuable read for you). Feeling stressed as a new teacher is about as normal as winter being cold in Michigan... you can count on it 100% of the time. In fact, if you're a new teacher, and you're not stressed and feeling overwhelmed, then my guess is you're doing something drastically wrong!

My first couple years as a teacher were incredibly stressful. My mentor teacher wasn't Yoda by any stretch of the imagination. He'd assign essays to the kids, then not ever read them. He'd let kids play cards in his History class. Don't get me wrong, I learned a lot from him, but it was what not to do. It wasn't until my 4th or 5th year of teaching, at a fantastic school in Detroit (University Prep Panther for life!), that I finally considered myself competent and skilled as a classroom teacher. Sure, I was 'good enough' before that. My kids generally behaved, I got through the textbook, students were mildly engaged, etc. But let's be honest... 'good enough' just isn't good enough when it comes to our students.

So I learned new techniques, changed my mindset, changed my focus, did a quick stint as an administrator (that's a whole different beast, for another book), and eventually landed in California as an Academic Coach and Professor in a Teacher Prep Program. Over all those years and all those experiences, I slowly tested ideas, keeping what worked, discarding the fads and gimmicks that didn't. Finally, as a grizzled old vet, I can honestly say I am able to confidently guide new teachers through that tough beginning period, and set them up for future success, and much faster growth as a professional than I ever experienced.

The question now became.... How? How do I spread the wealth? That's where the seed for this book took root. Why sit around and wait for new teachers to ask me for advice, when most of them are too nervous to ask for help anyway, afraid others will think they're not cut out for teaching? Why settle for a position where I get to work with teachers at one or two different campuses? Let's get the word out there and help the most teachers in the least amount of time! I've learned a lot over the last 18 years of teaching, what to do and what not to do. And as a wise 'man' once said: *"Pass on what you have learned" -Yoda.*

Teaching is teaching. Whether you're teaching 1st grade, 11th grade, college, or fellow educators, it's the same mindset. Teaching isn't the delivery of information, it's the teaching of skills - the empowering of the student to become more independent. That's what this book will aim to do for you, that's what I do through my relationship with my coaching clients, and that's what you've been called to do as a teacher.

But let's be honest, that's the fluffy, high-minded, philosophical definition of teaching. That's what got you fired up as an undergrad, and lured you into this profession. That's what you imagined your days would be.... like 'Dead Poet Society' or something.

We live in the real world however. And here, in the real world, that's only one slice of the teaching pizza. Let's not forget grading papers, lesson plans, staff meetings, union meetings, parent conferences, room setup, room setup again, room cleanup, professional developments (cringe), etc etc. Somewhere in all that, you're also supposed to inspire the future generation.

Needless to say, once you're knee deep in your first year of teaching (mid-September, once the honeymoon period has ended), you're going to be feeling overwhelmed. You're going to need a little assistance, whether you think so or not, whether you know where to look for it or not.

And lucky for you, you're holding it. Right here, in your hands, is a handy dandy guide to help you survive that wonderfully chaotic calling you've answered. Will this book make you a Master Teacher overnight? Will it impart all the wisdom and knowledge I've learned over 18 years of teaching K-12 and college?

Oh god no. Not even close.

What it will do is keep your head above water while you learn how to swim on your own.

So sit back, get some note paper, and perhaps an adult beverage or two, and let me guide you through the Dos and Don'ts of the first year of your teaching career.

Don't worry. We'll get you through this.

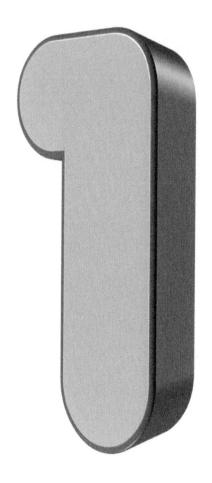

Chapter 1
It's Not Personal

You're driving home from work on a typical day at school, and all you can think is which bottle of wine you're going to crack open. It's been one of those days that drains you completely. Not physically, but emotionally. Maybe that one student, the one who knows exactly how to grab onto that last nerve of yours, said something especially mean and hurtful. Maybe your colleague down the hall, who's supposed to be mentoring you, has yet to give you any decent advice. Maybe your principal popped into your room to observe, and just stood there writing on a clipboard, not speaking a word. Or maybe it was that most dreaded event, the negative parent phone call, with yet another mom or dad wondering why you've been picking exclusively on their little angel.

Whatever it was that has given you that crushed-soul feeling, you're starting to question if this is all worth it. Everyone seems so eager to take things out on you! What did you do to incur their wrath?

The answer is simple: <u>nothing</u>.

None of it has to do with you, none of it is because of you, and none of it is your fault. Allow me to explain.

Students

It always seems to be on the days when everything starts out so well, that *it* happens. The line at Starbucks was nice and short, the traffic was light, and the janitor even did a stellar job cleaning up that spilled juice on your classroom rug from the day before. Everything seems to be going your way. Yes, it's on those days, when that one student comes to school, hell bent on treating you like garbage, making you their personal punching bag.

Maybe he curses at you. Maybe he tells you he hates you. Maybe he does everything in his power to purposefully derail your lesson (you know it's on purpose, because he's grinning at you while he's throwing things at his neighbor). Whatever it is, you just can't seem to figure out WHY. You look in the mirror and think "What did I do to this kid? What did I do wrong?" And understandably, like any normal human being, you feel bad afterwards. Both because another person was super rude to you (even if they are only 12), and because you feel like you've failed at your job.

Then, if it's really bad, you start thinking those thoughts that all veteran teachers have allowed to creep into their mind from time to time: that this is just a 'bad kid'.

The term 'bad kid' (or similar variations) blows around like autumn leaves in almost every teachers lounge in America. It's easy to just write the kid off as a bad seed, even when you're doing everything in your power to make a positive impact. I mean, why else would a human act like that?! Whether the parents really screwed this one up, or they were born with an extra helping of brat DNA, why not just pull the plug on trying with this one?

I'll tell you why. Because it's not YOUR fault, and it's not THEIR fault either.

A wise educator once told me "No child wakes up in the morning and decides to be an a-hole." There is a reason that student is acting out the way they are. You don't know what that reason is, and you may never know it. But that doesn't mean it's not there, and that it's not significant.

For example, that student might live in fear at home, fear of abuse (mental or physical), fear of hunger, etc. And they might be afraid to express that fear because they have learned through experience that their home is not a safe place. Where's the one place they feel safe? Your classroom.

A logical, emotionally well-adjusted, reasonable adult would argue that one wouldn't intentionally sabotage the one safe place one has in their life, by acting out. But these aren't adults, and they sure aren't logical. They are children, with brains that are by no means developed, and depending on the grade you teach, they have a cocktail of hormones rushing through their veins that would make anyone dizzy.

Is it fair that they treat you so horribly on an almost daily basis? Is it right? Of course not. But we accepted the calling to be teachers to help children. If you've been wasting any of your time worrying about 'fair', just stop worrying right now.

To be fair, this is easier said than done. It's easy for my type "don't take it personally" right now, but when you're in the thick of things, it's difficult to remember that. It's difficult to remind yourself, in the middle of that student flare-up, that this has nothing to do with you. I still struggle with reminding myself, and probably always will. But it's so important that we do.

Parents

This category is a tough one. When we become teachers, we obviously prepare ourselves to work with children. We know we'll have fellow teachers around us who can be less than professional or supportive, that's natural in any work environment. And we've heard stories of principals (good and bad) from teachers we know. But rarely is anyone prepared for that 4th group of people, a group that's so critical to the success of our teaching career: parents.

There are endless memes online making fun of different types of parents, even with catchy terms like Helicopter Parents, Lawnmower Parents, etc. At the end of the day, this is the group that teachers would most likely describe as the most irritating. Why? Because of their inability to see their child as being anything less than an angel. I mean, come on! Anyone who's spent more than 5 minutes with little Bobby knows he's a terror, what's wrong with Bobby's mom? Why does she keep defending him?

The key to understanding this group is no different than the students: empathy. There is a reason mom refuses to admit little Bobby's terrorism of your class. There's a reason she tries to blame everyone under the sun besides him. She's not blind. She knows. Deep down, when she's by herself at home, she admits it to herself. But you'll probably never hear that admission, and that's fine. You'll probably never hear the reason she won't admit to you what you and her already know.

But we are here to help our students, not exact a pound of flesh from a parent we blame for giving us Bobby every morning. Bobby isn't going anywhere, and neither is mom. So, at the end of the day, we have to let the 'why' go, and focus on the 'how'. How do we move forward? How do we just 'let it go' and focus on a solution. Remember this phrase, which I'll use often and explain later in the book: 'play offense.' Don't let the circumstance dictate to you. You dictate the circumstances.

It is essential (and I'll expand on this concept in a later chapter) to realize that everyone, EVERYONE, has their own personal kryptonite. Everyone has that one thing that you as a teacher can use, to disarm their negative behaviors, and lead them onto a more positive path. In this case, what is mom's kryptonite? It's Bobby. It's her undying, unrealistic love for her child. So, as the teacher (and many times the only 'adult' in the room), you need to find a way to get mom to believe you're just as crazy about her Bobby as she is. That comes down to <u>relationships</u>.

I'm going to tell you right now, there's no way around it, and there's no way to avoid it if you want to be a successful teacher: you must contact parents. Frequently. And you must do it for positive reasons. Mom can't see the school's number on her caller ID and automatically assume Bobby got in trouble. Naturally, she will be put into a defensive, negative mode before she even answers.

If you take time, at the very beginning of the year, to call your parents, email your parents, and show them you're a real person, who has nice things to say about their kid, you'll be stunned what a difference that'll make.

REAL WORLD POPUP

In a past year, I taught a couple twin brothers, who were not the most respectful in their classes. Early in the year, before I could even setup a meeting, I had to have a serious chat with one of the boys in the hall. He of course went home and told mom I 'yelled at him in front of everyone'. This obviously wasn't true, but it didn't matter, as it put mom on defense right away. I made a point of standing my ground on the matter (in a polite and respectful way of course), but then within the next week, looking for any genuine reason to call her again with a positive report.

All it took was once. As soon as she saw a teacher who was willing to see the good behavior with the bad (where most focused only on the bad), this mom became my biggest fan. Now, her sons' behavior improved in MY class (not others), because her boys saw their mother's respect for this one particular teacher, and it rubbed off.

So, see your parents as a resource, not the enemy. Build the relationships right away, and you'll avoid the frustrating meetings where they blindly defend their kids, because they'll trust you. After all, no one loves your students more than they do.

TRY THIS!

Here's an easy way to stay in contact with your parents that will build the foundation for a positive relationship, even before you meet them: Teacher Newsletter!

Using programs such as MailChimp, you can easily organize an email list for your parents, and use their pre-designed templates to create fun and unique emails the parents will love. Fill them with photos from class, updates on fun activities, and invitations to student presentations. You'll be infinitely more popular than your colleagues among the parents!

Teachers

Your fellow teachers... there are no greater resources, no better support system, and no more qualified shoulder to cry on. They understand. They know what you're going through, because they go through it too. If there's any group of people you can trust to have your back, it's your fellow teachers. Right??

Sort of.

I don't need to tell you that teaching is an incredibly stressful calling. That stress and pressure can bring out the best in people, especially naturally selfless people like teachers. But there are always exceptions, and in the teaching field, those exceptions can be glaring and crushing. Sometimes, just sometimes, a teacher becomes so negative and disheartened (again, like before, we may never know the reason why) that they're more than happy to throw you under the bus to further their own agenda. While you expect your colleagues to be Marcus Antonius, sadly there's sometimes a Brutus in the bunch, and we know how that turned out. (NOTE: If you don't know how that turned out, brush up on your Shakespeare already!)

It's one thing when a student upsets you or is rude to you, but when your own colleague talks smack about you, or throws you under the bus, that's a whole different level of betrayal.

Here's the good news with this particular group: they're easy to spot and easy to avoid. When little Bobby has it out for you, there's no avoiding him. You have to address that head on. When Mr Smith down the hall is being super negative, you can see that a mile away. When Mr Smith tries to get other teachers to get caught up in b$%ch sessions about the administration in the teacher's lounge, you can easily avoid him.

My advice for this group is just that: avoid them. This is the only group you can do that with. You can't avoid students (obviously) or parents (unless you want to make things worse), but avoid those 'Dementor Teachers' as I like to label them (see Harry Potter for reference). The danger in associating with a

Dementor Teacher, is that their negativity is contagious. Over time, you'll find yourself beginning to do the same things they do... complaining in the lounge about kids, labeling certain students as "bad ones", etc. Once that takes hold, you might as well retire or find a new career, because at that point, you'll be coming in just for the paycheck. And that type of teacher is never what our students need.

Administrators

The boss. The Big Cheese. The Head Honcho. The person you freak out about when they walk into your room with a clipboard. Teachers often see these menacing beasts as their nemesis, a cold-hearted automaton out to give them poor evaluations and force them to sit through boring PDs.

They're not.

Before you start throwing moldy tomatoes at me for being a traitor, let me explain. I'm not arguing that often administrators in some schools don't do things that infuriate their teaching staff. I'm not arguing that they don't often walk into classrooms with clipboards, and make your heart race and palms sweat. I'm simply arguing that most times their intention is not to make you feel nervous or frustrated. In fact, it's not about YOU at all.

The amount of pressure on administrators is incredible. While teachers talk about the pressure to have their kids perform well on standardized tests, let's face it, if they don't, the hammer is much more likely to fall on school administration than on the individual teachers. Teachers are protected by tenure and their unions in most cases. Administration is not, and can be axed at the drop of a hat by an angry school board.

Think of them as the over-stressed parent, who has way too much on their mind.

If you're a parent you know what this is like. You may come across as cold, distant, and aloof. But it's really just because you have so much stress on your mind that you don't even notice the reactions of the people around you.

So when they walk into your room, smile, and have a student welcome them in. It'll be a much more pleasant experience for them, and by association, you.

Last Word

The pressure of being a teacher is incredible. There's no need to add extra, imagined pressures to the already daunting real pressures. This might be the toughest lesson that I had to learn, and even now I struggle with it.... It's. Not. Personal.

Chapter 2
Plan, Plan, and then... Plan

Lesson Plans. In my opinion, there is no more valuable a tool for teachers. Period. And there is also not one thing more underutilized and avoided by teachers. Period.

Before we discuss what an excellent lesson plan looks like, or how to create one, let's make sure we're on the same page, and agree that they ARE important. If you don't think so, then you either need to have a serious change of heart before continuing, or it's time to lend this book to a friend. Because some things in this chapter are bound to offend.

Think of it this way. You have this great house in the country, and the view out of the back windows is amazing. Wouldn't it be a wonderful idea to have a huge, multi-level deck built along the back of the house? Think of all the family gatherings back there! Think of the romantic evenings, sipping wine and watching the sun set. So, you get all excited, find a contractor that everyone says is really nice (though you haven't actually seen his work), and hire him to start. The contractor shows up on the first day with his tools and equipment, and starts heading to the backyard immediately. You feel puzzled. So, you flag him down and ask "Excuse me... we didn't talk about a plan for the deck. Do you have any blueprints? Any drawings of the finished product?"

"Nah" he responds "I'll just wing it. I've been doing this a while. Don't worry."

There is no way you'd allow him to start working. Yet, teachers who don't use well crafted lesson plans are doing the same thing: winging it. And they're winging it with something far more important than a deck, they're winging it with the minds of our youth.

"But I've been teaching the same thing for twenty years! I can do this with my eyes closed." you might hear from your veteran colleagues. First, I'd question any teacher who has been using the same lesson for twenty years. But beyond that, each group of students has unique strengths and challenges, and requires unique approaches to your teaching and lessons. To give a one size fits all lesson, is simply to give up on good teaching, and take the lazy way out. (I told you some people might get offended).

The Plan

Now that I've browbeat you into agreeing that lesson plans are essential for any teacher worth their salt, the question remains, "What makes a good lesson plan?" To that question, there's the short answer, and the long answer. Let's begin with the short answer.

A good lesson plan.... Is one that you actually use.

I know that's not very specific, and teachers hate vague answers, but let me explain. Often teachers are asked to write lesson plans by their administrators. They do, just to keep from getting in trouble. They usually use a format that the site or district has decided, in their infinite wisdom, is the 'correct format', and will change everyone's lives for the better. So, the teacher sits down on their prep hour, fills in all the appropriate blanks on the assigned lesson plan template, and sends it off to their administrator, never to be seen by human eyes again.

Yes, that description is a bit depressing, and a tad pessimistic, but sadly it's all too common. When lesson plans are treated like an assignment by administration, they are done like assignments by teachers; turned in because they have to, and to avoid getting in trouble. This is an absolute waste of time for everyone involved. The teachers are blindly filling in spaces on a template, without doing the deep thinking of how their classroom can be organized, and learning promoted, by having an intentional plan in place. Administration gets a flood of emails with attached plans, that they have neither the time to review, nor often the training to assess. And the students (remember them?) end up with frustrated teachers who just wasted a chunk of valuable time doing something other than thinking about them and their learning experiences.

How can teachers take control of the lesson plan process, and use it as the powerful tool it is? It would be helpful if their administration didn't treat it as an assignment, though that's not in the teacher's sphere of influence. Allowing teachers to create (or borrow) lesson plan formats gives them ownership over the product and the process, and increases the likelihood that they'll actually use them. Often, progressive districts will allow "freedom within a frame" when it comes to writing lesson plans. They will give a list of 'common aspects' that every teacher must include in their plans (see the next subsection), but as long as those parts are included, the format and any additional pieces are completely up to the individual teacher. This creates a wide variety among staff, as far as layouts and styles, but since lesson plans are supposed to be for the teacher's use, that doesn't matter much.

If that freedom isn't granted by a district, teachers have no choice but to create lesson plans using the district assigned format. If this is the case, there are two options left for the teacher: 1) Get used to the school assigned format, and learn to like it, or 2) turn in that format, set it off to the side, then rewrite it in a format you'll really use.

But that's double the work, Dino!

Yes, I know, I know. But while being assigned a lesson plan format you won't use is a tough position to be in, it's far more valuable to create two copies and have one you'll use, as opposed to creating one copy and having nothing to use in your classroom.

So what does a good lesson plan actually have in it? That brings us to the long answer. A good lesson plan... contains the following components:

- Objective
- Standards
- Assessments (daily)
- Teacher instruction
- Student practice

While there are plenty of other components you can add to a lesson plan, these 5 are essential. A lesson plan that is missing any one of these is incomplete, and lacking in the depth necessary to ensure your students are engaged and learning. Let's break down each part:

1. ***Objective:*** One or two sentences, with a <u>measurable</u> verb ("students will know" is not measurable, but "Students will describe the 3 causes" is measurable), written in <u>student-friendly</u> language (so the students understand what's going on), that describe the <u>goal</u> (and point) of the lesson. We all know those kids who ask "What's the point of this?", the Objective answers that question. And in all honesty, if you can't explain what the point

of the lesson is, should you really be teaching it?

2. **_Standards:_** If there's one thing that ties all teachers' lessons together, it's the standards, both content and literacy standards. If your lessons aren't focused, in some way, toward one of your standards, then that's obviously an issue.

3. **_Assessments (daily):_**
There's a reason I included the term 'daily' next to assessments. Assessments are so much more than tests or quizzes. In fact, formative assessments should a common piece of all your lessons. How can you be confident your students will succeed, or are even learning, if you're not assessing on a daily

basis? Exit tickets, quick checks, class discussions, etc are all useful formative assessments.

4. ***Teacher instruction:*** Most of the time, we plan parts of a lesson to make sure we are doing enough of something. In the case of 'teacher instruction' we often need to make sure we aren't overdoing it. As a secondary History teacher, I can speak with experience. We often love our content so much, we inadvertently find ourselves yapping on and on, only to look up and realize the class stopped listening a long time ago. Don't be that teacher. Plan exactly what you're going to say, and don't add to the plan.

5. ***Student practice:*** No matter what your grade level, and no matter what subject area, student practice is an essential part of any lesson. It's where the students show what they've (hopefully) learned, make it their own, and burn it into their brains. Don't ever skip this section. Otherwise you're just the boring teacher from Ferris Bueller's Day Off. ("Anyone.... anyone...")

Or, in a more simplified, logical flow:

1. *What's the goal of my lesson?*

2. *What standard(s) will it address?*

3. *How will I know the students met the goal?*

4. *What will I do during the lesson?*

5. And what will the students do?

If you can answer those 5 questions, you have the beginnings of a solid instructional lesson. It won't matter what format or template you use, what boxes you check off, etc. Those are the core to any good classroom lesson, and should be present on every lesson plan you write.

REAL WORLD POPUP

Don't skip over formative assessments. So many teachers focus on the big tests and quizzes, they fail to catch learning gaps as they're happening on a daily basis. One example of a simple and quick formative assessment, that quickly became a zero-pressure routine in my classroom, was the "Thumb-O-Meter". At any point in class, no matter what we were discussing, I could stop and say "Fists in the air!" (Kids all raise their fists) "Thumb up if you're feeling good about what we're discussing, thumb sideways if you could use a little more clarification from me, and thumb down if Mr Mangano is making no sense at all and needs to try again." The key to making this zero-pressure, is the intentional wording of the 'thumb sideways' and 'thumb down' options. I am placing the reason for the gap in understanding on my explanation, not on their lack of comprehension. I still get the formative assessment I need, but without making any students feel like they are at fault for their confusion.

But They're Already Done For Me...

I think it's important to address another elephant in the room. This pesky pachyderm is the one disguised and a hand set of lesson plans already created for you. Sometimes they even have all the parts listed above. Many times however, they're a simple calendar or pacing guide. Why can't we just use those, especially if they're supplied by the textbook company, the same book you're told to use anyway?

Because they're not YOUR lessons, created for YOUR students. Those plans were created without knowing the reading levels of your kids, without realizing their 3 day plan would take 5 or 6 in your class, because your kids love to break into debates. Sure you can use them as a starting point, but they still need to be personalized for your classes.

As for pacing guides... they are not lesson plans, and should never be used as a substitute for them. A pacing guide might give you a general topic for the day, but lacks any of the nuances needed to navigate your individual goals for your classes, and rarely involve formative assessments, teacher vs student activities, etc.

TRY THIS!

Writing daily objectives is time consuming enough as it is. Trying to make sure they're "student friendly" makes it even tougher.

Try writing your classroom objectives WITH you kids! Not only does it give them ownership on the teaching/learning process, but it is also a great reading comprehension activity in itself. Always look for a way to sneak in more literacy!

Last Word

Lesson plans... the most important use of your time on a Sunday afternoon while you favorite football team is losing. In all seriousness though, proper planning is the most powerful, <u>proactive</u> thing you can do to ensure you have a smooth week. I learned the hard way with this one (see a pattern here).

Chapter 3
Get Some Help Already

We all know that one teacher who the school affectionately calls 'The Hermit'. They do their own thing, and might be a good teacher, but don't ask for help from anyone, nor do they offer to help their colleagues. They lock themselves in their room, pile up the proverbial sand bags, and hunker down to 'be left alone'. As a veteran teacher, they may think that works fine for them (I'd argue that point, but that's a different topic). But that simply will not do for a new teacher. In fact, I'd argue that finding a new teacher who doesn't need to seek out assistance, would be like finding a leprechaun riding a unicorn.... Good luck with that.

As stated earlier, and as is the main reason for even writing this book, one could argue that more than any other profession in America today, teachers are the least prepared coming out of college. To think that the courses filled with theory, term papers, and a complete lack of real world experience, will properly prepare a teacher for the endless variety of unexpected hiccups that occur in a school year, is somewhat ridiculous. The student teaching experience helps, but only so much as training wheels help a child learn to ride a bike. The knowledge of that safety net is always there, and keeps the new teacher's stress level down. Being in your own classroom, as a first year teacher, without the training wheels of your mentor teacher being in the room with you, is a daunting reality that can't be simulated. Also, the quality of the mentor teacher's support makes a huge difference as well. The mentor might be a fantastic classroom teacher, but maybe doesn't focus enough time and attention on their apprentice teacher. Or, what happened to me, the mentor teacher offers more damaging advice than helpful advice, and can be a detriment to the mentee.

So the wise first year teacher realizes, unlike the hermit teacher, that they need the assistance of their colleagues. They understand that they can only be better served from the experience of finding help in other, more experienced educators.

But who should they ask? How do they reach out?? Where to begin? Being a new teacher is stressful enough. Having to go find help is just one more thing to add to the already unmanageable To-Do list. Schools are supposed to assign each new teacher a mentor teacher, someone who checks in once in a while (usually every 2 weeks) to make sure everything's going ok. But ask anyone who's been in the business for a while, and they'll tell you, this rarely ever happens how it's supposed to. Take for instance, a school I worked at before. It was a small school, with around 20 teachers. Perhaps 4 teachers were brand new, 1st year teachers. Maybe another 4-5 were in their first 3 years (still relatively green). While technically they planned to assign a mentor teacher to each new teacher (they were legally required to), and planned to hire an Instructional Coach to support all the newer teachers (which was a great idea), neither happened. As the year went on, and more and more excuses piled up, it became evident to all the staff that they were on their own. The administration promised to take on the coaching role, but never did. They'd have to find their own mentors. They'd have to find their own answers to pressing classroom challenges. At the end of the day, no matter what reasons were given, or how legitimate they were, the teachers ended up suffering. That in turn, means the students ended up suffering.

Situations like this are sadly commonplace, and so it's necessary to be able to find your own resources as needed, and be eternally grateful if your school supports you properly.

First, get to know your colleagues. I mean, really get to know them, as instructors. Start up conversations about best practices. Ask them what they're teaching this week. And most importantly, ask to observe their classroom. There is no quicker way to become a seasoned teacher, than to observe one. If you have to go during your prep hour, do so. It's a valuable use of that time. Stay for the entire lesson, and take note of every teacher move they make, from how they greet the kids, to how they move around the room, to how they deal with problem behavior. If they share the same prep period as you, ask your administration to cover you for one period so you can go observe. Because so few teachers ever ask for that, most administrators would be pleasantly stunned, and bend over backwards to make it happen for you.

REAL WORLD POPUP

When I was a brand new teacher, the mentor teacher who was assigned to me was, let's just say, less than professional. Almost everything I learned from him, was what <u>not</u> to do. He would assign these incredibly long essays to the kids, and when they'd finally write them and turn them in, he'd wait until they left the room, and grade them by weight! He'd hold one in his hand, bob it up and down, and say "That feels like a B+." Little did the students know, he never read a single one. He also taught an elective class I was dying to teach, but because he had seniority, he had first pick. Yet, in the class, many days he just let the kids play cards! I knew this because those kids would come to my class and ask to continue the game they started in

---

his. But there was one thing he did teach me (intentionally) that was valuable: Play Offense. What he meant by that, was to plan ahead when it came to classroom culture, and keep control of the room, forcing the students to adapt to your expectations. Don't react to student behaviors, and constantly change your practice based on their behavior.

Second, there's this fantastic thing called the internet, filled with countless discussion boards of teachers looking to support one another. Just on Facebook alone, I joined so many that I had to leave some, because I couldn't keep up with all the rich discussions. Simpy go to Facebook, search "new teachers", filter to just "groups", and you'll be in business.

And let's not forget the website TeachersPayTeachers. While many of the resources on this site cost money (thus the name) there is a decent collection of freebies. This site has quickly become the go-to place online to get some really creative lesson ideas.

However, nothing can compare to an individual Instructional Coach. An Instructional Coach works with you, and is focused 100% on helping you become the best teacher you can be. Instructional Coaches are not a new concept, but only recently have school districts begun to realize their value, and set aside the resources to make them a permanent fixture in schools.

If you are lucky enough to teach at a school that has an Instructional Coach... first say a prayer of thanks, then run, don't walk, to their office and schedule a time to meet. This person needs to quickly become your best friend on campus. Too often, Instructional Coaches are looked at with distrust by teachers. They think the coaches are 'spies' for the administrators, or are actually administrators themselves! This couldn't be further from the truth. A true coach is someone who meets you where you are, on your terms, and guides without judging. In fact, many coaches have a strict rule of not being able to tell the administration anything about the teachers they meet with! That way, you can feel comfortable in being vulnerable and open is discussing your struggles, and they can help you solve your challenges much more successfully.

If your school isn't enlightened yet, and doesn't have an Instructional Coach on staff, I'd highly suggest hiring your own. Before you even think "But I can't afford that, I'm a new teacher!", let me assure you, there are plenty of coaches out there who can tailor a coaching plan to fit just about any budget. And since more and more Instructional Coaches offer online coaching, not only is the cost even less, but it widens the pool of coaches available to you. Heck, there's even a coach like that writing the book you're currently reading (go check out the last page)!

TRY THIS!

There are countless coaches online, who you don't need to even be in the same country as in order for them to help you. Find ones that will offer "free consultations". While these are a way for the coaches to gain your trust (and your business), they're also extremely helpful for the teacher, as many of the consultations are planning conversations that assist you in clarifying what you really need support in. That may look very different than what you initially think.

Look in the credits at the end of the book for one such coach.

If coaching seems like a foreign concept to you as a teacher, you're not alone. However, teachers are college educated professionals, just like business professionals, medical professionals, etc. They commonly have professional coaches in their fields. Why should a teacher, who's responsible for a room full of young minds, be any different?

Last Word

(Double negative alert): Don't think you don't need help. You do. We all do. It's best if you embrace that reality now, and get support on this incredible, exhausting roller coaster ride. Get a coach, grab a colleague, use your administration, but whatever you do, find someone who's knowledgeable, trustworthy, and available, to guide you whenever you need it.

Chapter 4
The Cool Teacher

Respect. There are plenty of wise sayings about respect. "Respect is earned, not given", etc. There is no need for me to list a bunch of them here, you can go find your own if you want. The point is, respect is key for any new teacher starting their school year. Too often, new teachers desperately want their students to like them. Schools are filled with bright eyed new teachers, who've been dreaming of being that 'cool teacher' they see in movies. But that shouldn't be the goal, as it won't get you what you ultimately want, which is a positive classroom culture. Instead, new teachers should be laser focused on earning the students respect, as opposed to their friendship. That however, can be a long and messy process if not done properly.

The trap of trying to get students to 'like you' is a common one, and if you want your students to actually learn, and want your classroom to look like an actual classroom, you must avoid it at all costs.

"Wait a minute Dino! You're saying I should not want my students to like me?!" Not exactly. It shouldn't be your GOAL that they like you. Your GOAL should be a positive classroom environment where students are able to learn. That goal is attained by focusing on respect, not friendship. While it's tempting to take the easier, 'friendship route', this is (as Admiral Akbar would say), a trap.

Here is a short list of temptations to avoid:

1. **Letting your students break school rules**
   "I know we're not supposed to have snacks in class, but go ahead. Just put

them away really fast if the admin comes in."

"Sure, you can wear your hat in my class, just don't tell other teachers I let you."

These are real quotes from colleagues of mine in the past. It's tempting to let students ignore some of the more innocent rules, ones that won't really hurt anyone if they're broken. I mean, it's not like you're allowing them to Greco-Roman wrestle in class. The problem with this logic, is that students don't make that distinction. They place teachers in one of two camps:

1) Teachers I can get my way with, and

2) Teachers I have to listen to.

So, without realizing it, by just allowing simple things like eating snacks in class when they aren't supposed to, you're infecting your students with a bad case of Argue-itis, and they will push you on any and every rule they don't want to follow. Draw the line once, in the beginning, and save yourself a year of headaches. This is so much easier to do when you start the year consistent, as opposed to starting lax, then trying to 'tighten things up' later in the year.

TRY THIS!

Enforcing class rules can be a year long, unending siege if the rules aren't purposeful. Try creating the class rules together as a class, in the first week of school. Let the students create most of them, while holding the 'veto power' as the teacher. You'll be surprised how, with the proper guidance, the students are able to create some pretty impressive, positive class norms.

Also, because the students have a feeling of ownership in the class rules, they are far more inclined to follow those rules without prompting, and definitely without argument.

2. *Acting unprofessional around your students*

This one always makes me laugh, because I've fallen victim to this temptation a few times, and made a fool out of myself. I feel like I came across as Dr Evil in the first Austin Powers movie, "I'm cool! I'm hip!" Speaking their lingo, playing their music, dressing overly casual, etc are all things that are just fine, after a solid teacher/student relationship is built. Once they've learned where your limits are, that it's your classroom 100% of the time, and they should never mistake your kindness for weakness, then joking around with them is a wonderful way to solidify that already professional relationship. But stay professional. Don't take it too far, such as slipping in a curse word to show how 'real' you are. You'll only be sabotaging your own authority.

3. *Letting deadlines slide*
   This temptation, if succumbed to, will really piss off your coworkers! Imagine an essay is due on Friday. On Friday, you want to make them all happy, and give them an extension over the weekend. They cheer, they applaud, they erect statues in your honor. They go to their next class and give their next teacher hell, because he didn't give them an extension. It. Happens. Every. Time. Also, the extension policy will become,

in their minds, the norm. You'll be met with all kinds of arguing when the next assignment isn't given an extension. If your students are having a tough time meeting deadlines, teach them time management strategies. Don't give them more time.

4. **Keeping poor behavior secret from parents and/or administration**

Because parents can be such a complicated dimension of teaching on their own, deciding when and how to inform them of student misdeeds is doubly complicated. It is important that students don't ever think you play favorites, and the best way to screw that up is to have the "OK, this time I won't call home, but promise not to do it again" conversation with a student. No matter how private it is, no matter how much they promise not to tell their classmates, word will spread like wildfire. It's a school. The certainty is 100%. And once that gets around, you are going to hear it from all sides.... Kids, teachers, and worst of all, that parent who is pissed that you withheld that info from them.

The easiest way to avoid this trap? Have a policy, and stick to it. If X, Y, or Z happen, parents are automatically called. Make that clear to students ahead of time, so if 'the call' goes home, they have only themselves to blame. And heck, they might even learn some personal responsibility in the process.

At the end of the day, you are going to spend a LOT of time with this group of children, more time than with most other people in your life. Humans, being social animals, tend to resemble those they spend the most time with. So, either they will start to emulate you over a long period of time, or if you're not careful, you'll start emulating them. Would you rather the former be true, where they start speaking and writing in complete sentences, showing grit by working through difficult challenges, or even (gasp) wearing a collared shirt once in a while, all in an attempt to be a little more like the teacher they've learned to <u>respect?</u> Or, will you continue to try and impress them, by acting like them, thus teaching them that it's OK for adults to do the things and say the things they do?

REAL WORLD POPUP

At a past school, one of the worst problems (and this will sound silly) we had was the wearing of hats. It wasn't because it was tough to enforce, but because only some teachers enforced it. If every teacher enforced it, students would know there were exactly <u>zero</u> classes they could wear their sweet new cap in, and would leave it home.

But because 3 of their 7 teachers didn't care, they'd carry hats around in their hands, wearing and removing them as they could get away with it. Imagine a giant game of Whack-A-Mole, but with teens wearing hats. I actually developed quite a sneaky, silent technique of snatching a hat from a head, from behind, without making any contact with anyone. They never saw 'Mr Mangano: Hat Ninja' coming!

The answer is simple when put in those terms. However, nothing is ever that cut and dry during an average school day, and without other veteran teachers pointing these things out, you might not have even thought about this. Or, maybe you thought being the 'cool teacher' was the right way to go about building relationships. Maybe you have colleagues who are that 'cool teacher', and you're envious of them, seeing all the kids chatting with them in the hall, "kickin it" with them, meanwhile you are getting an evil-eye when they walk by your room.

Keep the faith. There are one of two things true about that cool colleague. Either it's an act in the hallway, and their classroom is really run by the kids (not in a good way), or they were a consistent, high-standards teacher early on, and now the students actually respect them. That's why they're "showin' the love" during passing time.

Be that second teacher.

Because that's the natural end to that progression: the more the students learn to respect you as an adult and a teacher, the more they'll want to talk to you, learn from you,and be in your classroom. Before you know it, people will see YOU as that cool teacher, and you'll have earned it, the right way.

Last Word

R.E.S.P.E.C.T. Find out what that means... for your classroom.

Earn that respect instead of trying to be liked, and your classroom, as well as your long-term reputation and career, will be better off for it.

Chapter 5
It's Not About You
(*and yet it is*)

I used to be one of those teachers who would make my classroom feel like home, an extension of my house. I'd have posters of things I liked, photos of friends and family hanging on the wall, my guitar in the corner, etc. I'd set my room up in the summer, before school started, and think to myself, "Man, this looks awesome!"

Then when the kids would arrive I'd stand there, all excited, waiting for them to fall in love with what I setup "for them"... and they never did. One or two kids would like my setup, but the rest would just shrug, and sit down, as if I gave them a plain white, sterile room, not the Palace of Awesomeness I spent so long creating.

What I didn't realize then, and do now, is that my focus was inward, not pointed toward my kids and what they wanted/needed.

This example is a surface level, environmental one. But it's used to illustrate a mindset that exists when teachers plan how to TEACH as well, not just set up furniture, plants and posters.

Let's apply this same mindset to a lesson. As an Instructional Coach, my biggest challenge was getting History teachers to even admit there was anything about their lessons that needed improving. I'd walk into the room, the teacher would be lecturing *at* the class, their PowerPoint slides would be flashing by on their SmartBoard, the students were all silent... it was exactly what the teacher wanted and envisioned a classroom should be.

Yet, if one took the time to view this class from a student's point of view, they'd see students doing anything other than being engaged in the lesson. Students were sleeping, doodling, listening to headphones, texting their friends, etc. Even students who might have found History class enjoyable, were bored out of their mind. What the teacher needed was a silent audience where he could talk about History topics to his heart's content. What the students needed was an opportunity to interact with each other, and they got none of that.

Let's take this mindset to an even deeper example. In every single school I've been at so far, there is always one or two students who do absolutely no work whatsoever. They come in the room, and immediately shut down (head down, headphones in, etc). No matter how engaging my lessons might be (and I've come up with some awesome stuff over the years, if I do say so myself), no matter how much the rest of the class is into what we're doing, this one student won't lift their head off the desk. As a teacher, I might get frustrated. "I need my kids to participate, I need my kids to not checkout."

But what does this student need? Who knows? Well, if I keep focusing on myself, I sure won't know.

I may tell myself what I need is a classroom with 100% engaged students. But what I should be asking myself, is what does this student need, that he's not getting? It might be that he hasn't had a decent night's sleep in over a week. It might be that he hasn't eaten since yesterday's school lunch. He might be depressed. Homeless. Abused. What he needs is an adult who cares about him as a person, not an adult who needs an assignment turned in by the end of the hour.

Your students' needs will be as diverse and multiple as the stars in the night sky.

You'll always feel like you can't possibly keep up with their emotional needs, outside of the classroom. This doesn't change as you become a veteran, you only become a little more adept at juggling them.

Bobby needs to put his head down for the first few minutes of class to get his mind right, Michelle has been living on a friend's couch for the last few weeks, and doesn't eat breakfast, so you remember to bring her a granola bar. Steven is angry again this morning, and needs 5 minutes in the hall to release a little pressure, so he doesn't do it in class, etc. And this is before you've started teaching anything.

TRY THIS!

Sometimes what a student needs is just some time to be alone, especially our older kids. Try having a place in the room, away from

---

everyone else, where students can go sit and
be alone for 5 minutes, no questions asked...
a "chill chair".

As an example, just outside my classroom, we
are currently building/planting a small
garden full of cherry tomato plants, and a
bench in the middle, for just that use. It's a
student project, where she envisions kids
who are upset can sit and relax, and pick and
eat tomatoes until the feel better.

So, it's about your kids and their needs.
They can't take care of their educational
business unless they've dealt with their
personal and emotional business. And they'll
need your help for that. They deserve your
help. You owe them your help. Help in
learning how to control their emotions. Help
in managing their time. Help in putting their
pride to the side and asking for breakfast from

an adult who cares (you), and knowing they won't be judged.

"But" you may ask, "how on earth can I possibly do all that, and be all those things, for so many kids? I'll lose my mind! I'll burn out before I finish my first year!"

That's where the second part of this chapter's title comes in, "and yet it is". If we were to sum up all the different things I've said kids need <u>from</u> you in the past few pages, we see that what they really need <u>is</u> you. If you are what they really need, no matter who the student is and what their circumstances are, your top priority, if you really want to help them, is to be there.

Be there.

Be there in person. Be there emotionally. Be there mentally.

REAL WORLD POPUP:

Years ago, I had a student who had a very rough home life. This young lady lived with her mom, who was less than a stellar parent. When she entered her senior year, and was approaching graduation, another teacher and I started talking with her about graduating. We were concerned because she seemed to be self sabotaging. It turns out, her mom was encouraging her to dropout of school, and to start earning money (illegally) instead. The other teacher and I, in order to keep her motivated, ended up doing all the things for her that her mom should have... ordering her a prom dress, doing her Senior pictures, getting her cap and gown, etc. We needed to see her graduate, but what she needed was a parent. A real parent. We knew the only way we were going to get her on that stage at graduation was to become the parents she needed, but didn't have. And there have been many, many more examples like this over the years.

As I write this, it's mid-March (the Ides of March, for you Shakespeare buffs out there), and I am exhausted. I'm mentally, emotionally, and physically exhausted. There's nothing wrong, it's completely normal for a teacher to feel this way at this point of the year. This happened to be a long week, it's Friday, and so my gas tank is on empty. However, I am self-aware enough to recognize this, and to recognize that the worst thing for my students is for me to remain this way. The gas tank needs refilling, the old bones need a little rest. And so this weekend, I'll make a point of taking care of myself, so that I can take care of my students on Monday.

This might seem obvious, but don't underestimate how many teachers, especially new teachers, with all their youth and energy, burn the candle at both ends and end up crashing around this time of the school year. Teaching is draining enough, but when you see teachers try to juggle teaching with raising a family, with coaching a sport, with running an after school club... disaster is bound to strike. I've seen it time after time, teachers who don't prioritize their own mental and physical well-being, falling apart in the middle of a school year. And who suffers when that happens? The kids, of course. Forget the fact that those teachers have no energy left to even teach their classes in an engaging way, but how on earth can they give the extra emotional support to their most vulnerable students? They can't, and the students see that as plain as day.

__Last Word__

As they say at the beginning of every flight, put the air mask on yourself first before assisting others. Or, for the darker Star Wars fans out there, pretend your students are Boba Fett, when I paraphrase what he says "You're no good to me dead (on your feet)." Take care of yourself, so you can give the kids everything they need. It will be, inevitably, a whole lot.

Chapter 6
Painful Yet Worth It

NOTE: The purpose of this chapter is not to depress you, or make you cry. It's to make a point. A very necessary point, if you're going to enter this career with both eyes wide open. We will discuss the point later, but for now, go grab a tissue box.

Many years ago, we had a student in our school named 'Tom'. I met Tom during his 10th grade year, not because he was my student, which he wasn't, but because he often got into arguments with the boys in my class, who were a year older than him. Tom was a tall kid, definitely bigger than most of the other boys in the school. It seemed obvious to us that he felt the need to impose his size on others, as a way of coping with other issues. We were sure he was a 'bad kid' who was going to be a negative influence on our school. We'd come to find out later how wrong we were.

His 10th grade year went along, and there weren't many people who had positive experiences with Tom. Sure, his advisor insisted he was a good kid at heart, but we didn't believe it.

During his 11th grade year, our school planned a Team Building Camping Trip, consisting of 2 brave teachers (Mr. Pare and myself), and 8-10 male students who were in real danger of not graduating. The thought was, if we got them out into nature, away from the stresses of the city, and really built trusting relationships together, it might spark them when we returned to school. Naturally, Tom was invited.

To shorten a long story, Tom did great, and had a blast. He did the high ropes course (which is terrifying and thrilling at the same time), built his first campfire, expressed his innermost fears and insecurities, etc. Finally, on the last night, he and I were sitting by the fire he'd just built, and he said to me: "I think I'm going to go to college. And I want to go to a college that's away from a city, so I can build campfires and look at the stars any time I want." I really did start to tear up when he said that.

When we got back to school, not only did his behavior change, but his academics did too, as he now had a tangible goal in his life. By the time we did that trip the following year, he volunteered to be a counselor/mentor to the younger kids!

Interlude: At this point, I could end the story of Tom. It's beautiful, it's inspiring, and it's 100% true. It's also incomplete. This book isn't written to blow smoke up your backside, it's written to be honest and clear about what teaching is, what it REALLY is. And sometimes, like you've just read, it's the most amazing job. You can't believe people are paying you money to experience these things. But other times, it's gritty, heartbreaking, and... painful.

During Tom's senior year, he started applying to colleges. His grades weren't the best, but he had impressed so many teachers during his last 2 years, that he had a stack of recommendation letters.

Finally, one day, all 6'2", 300+ pounds of Tom came bounding down the hall like a deer, waving an acceptance letter from University of Arkansas Pine Bluff. He made it.

Tom's plan was to start school a semester later than normal (in January) so he could work and save up a little before going. Tom seemed to have an organized plan for everything! Tom eventually graduated, became one of the true success stories at our school (considering what he was like his 10th grade year), and went out into the world. We couldn't wait to see photos of him moving down to school in a few months.

Then, in November, about a month and a half before Tom was going to start at college, I got a call from Mr. Pare, the teacher who chaperoned with me on that camping trip.

"Tom's dead, Dino. He was shot last night."

The details aren't important, but out of respect for Tom and his memory, I will say that it wasn't his fault, he was truly in the wrong place at the wrong time, with the wrong people.

Go ahead and grab a tissue.

So, what's the point of telling you the story of Tom? I didn't make it up, it's 100%

true (except for his name of course). The point is, that hurt. That wasn't just a student of mine, that was a student I'd built campfires with, talked about life dreams with, heck, walked on ropes 30 ft in the air with. It was a student I helped plan his life with. I felt like my guts were ripped out, and I'm man enough to admit I cried like a baby after that phone call. I felt a lot of things, but one feeling was clear... I was DONE with teaching. This was too painful. Why on earth would I put myself through this misery of opening up my soul to kids only to have their lives cut short?

Often, when we make poor decisions, or think we want to go down a path we shouldn't, the Universe hears us, and says "Challenge Accepted". Why would I choose to risk that pain again? That question was answered when Mr. Pare and I attended Tom's funeral. Sure there were family and friends, but there were his classmates too. They were hurting as well. And when we got back to school the next day, they needed someone. Someone to talk with, someone to support them, someone to get them through the pain they were feeling.

I'll give you three guesses who that was.

So, what's the point of this admittedly depressing chapter? I want you, no <u>need</u> you, to understand that there are going to be times where being a teacher is going to hurt. That's the time when you have to fight the urge to pack it all up and get a job in a cubicle. Just wrap your mind around that now. It's not a matter of if, but when.

Sure, it might not be the same as what happened with Tom. But trust me, his is not the only funeral of a student I've been to. And it doesn't have to be losing a student that breaks your heart. It could be the student who's addicted to drugs by the age of 14. It could be the student you have to drive to a homeless shelter for the weekend, because the only way she'll qualify for a special college program is if she has paperwork proving she's been homeless. These have all happened, and I could go on.

TRY THIS!

We all care about our kids. Let's all showing our appreciation to them more often, in a more intentional way.

Try writing "appreciation notes" to them, randomly, for completely non-academic reasons. Write them to each and every one of your kids, not all at the same time, but a few per week. Many of your students have never had that kind of positive feedback from an adult before, and it might very well be the highlight of their year.

But for every time this job hurt, for
every time it breaks our heart, there are times
in which it lifts us up. Times when the Tom's
DO make it. That's where the next chapter
comes in. I am not so cruel as to end the book
on such a sobering (yet necessary) tone. Put
away your tissue, you'll be smiling your way
through Chapter 7.

Last Word

Teaching is wonderful, and painful.
Joyous and heartbreaking. Understanding
that it's not all hugs and gifted coffee mugs is
crucial to making it to the end of the marathon.

Chapter 7

It's Awesome Out Here

Whew! So far, this book has been pretty heavy. As a new teacher, you must be getting a little worried about what you've signed on for. That's why this last chapter is purposely positive, and filled with true stories from my teaching career so far, that have warmed my heart and kept me going.

This is in no way an exhaustive collection of these positive stories. In almost 20 years in secondary education I've lost count of all the times my students have made my job an absolute joy. You already read about one of them in the last chapter. Here are a few more tales, and I hope they convince you that even if this calling is tough, it's totally worth it (the stories are 100% true, only the names have been changed).

Kris

When I taught at UPREP High School in Detroit, we had an advisory system. We would follow the same group of teens for 2-4 years (depending on the cycle). In the autumn of 2007, I had just finished with my first advisory group (a challenging one), and was meeting my second group. This second group was a breath of fresh air in comparison... the students were mature, personable, and studious. I was super excited to be able to work with them for multiple years.

The exception to this rule was a young lady named Kris. Kris was a typical 9th grade girl, in that she thought her teacher was 'lame', and had no desire at first to build any kind of relationship. This wasn't an issue, as I knew students would initially be standoffish, until we spent time in class together.

As the first year went on, Kris started making a few poor decisions, as many 14 year olds do. However, one decision ended up being monumentally bad for her, and more life changing than she ever could have anticipated.

For the sake of avoiding details, it's enough to know that Kris made a poor decision with a male classmate, on campus. This isn't all that rare at that age. However, in Kris' case, the event made its way on the internet, and spread to the eyes of the entire campus faster than a wildfire. Kris was understandably devastated. In the days that followed, students were suspended, parents called in, etc. I remember sitting in the parent meeting with my principal, Kris, and her parents. This poor girl had definitely hit a low point.

However, things turned around for Kris, and quickly. She realized her decisions were a result of her low self esteem. She soon built positive relationships with the right peers, and with adults at school, including her advisor (me).

Not only did Kris rise from the emotional ashes like a teen version of the mythical phoenix, but she flourished. She graduated with excellent grades, and was accepted to a great university where she majored in counseling. Currently, she has earned a Master's Degree, and has made it her life mission to work with troubled and abused girls.

Through her journey, Kris and I became close while she was at our high school, and kept in touch while she was in college. She'd tell me from time to time that I played a crucial part in her getting through her rough early high school years, and while I appreciated the kid words, I knew better. I knew the credit was hers. She was a strong girl, who grew to be a strong woman. She could have crumbled, and let what happened during her freshman year define her. Many kids would have. She didn't. Words can't express how proud I am of this young lady, and I find myself smiling just writing this.

Beth

Back at that same school, there was another student, we'll call her Beth. Beth was one of those students who every teacher wanted to clone, and spread around the school. Great grades, great personality, professional and polite, etc. She even played soccer for me for a couple years. Then, graduation came. She got a full-ride scholarship to a university, and after graduation, she was on her way.

We kept in touch once in a while, and years later, she messaged me, with photos of her college graduation and a really sweet Thank You note. I looked at the photos, and smiled ear to ear. I noticed in many of the photos, she was holding a couple little boys. I asked if they were family. Her response blew me away: "No, those are my sons. I didn't really tell anyone I was pregnant because I didn't want any of my old teachers to think I might not finish college."

And not only did she finish, she finished in 4 years. Having twins didn't even slow her down a little.

She went on to her Masters Degree program, and not only did she marry her high school sweetheart, but I had the honor of doing the photography for the wedding.

Amy

Let me finish with the story of Amy. I met Amy during the very first substitute teacher job I had. I hadn't attended a single teacher prep course yet, and accepted a month long position subbing for an 8th grade ELA class. Needless to say, I had NO idea what the heck I was getting myself into.

The first thing I noticed was that the teacher left one week worth of plans, not one month. And since I had no idea what to do... I just winged it. We played ridiculous games, debated things, etc. One game was Silent Ball, a non-educational game that should be reserved for 2nd graders (yeah, it was embarrassing).

One young lady happened to be in that class twice a day, that was Amy. So she got a double dose of my ineptitude. However, she never complained, and was even helpful to the young, confused, ignorant sub who was wasting all their time.

Fast forward 2 years, and I accepted a teaching position at the high school in the same district. On the first day of school, Amy, now a sophomore, walked into my history class and said "Hey, it's Mr Mangano, the silent ball guy!" Of course it's THAT part of our time together that she remembered.

During that year, she became very close to two teachers, myself and a woman named Ms. Ameel. Amy had developed a negative attitude in life over the past two years, and it seemed we were the only two who had enough patience to see past that.

The following year, she became my student assistant, as well as Ms. Ameel's, and we all grew even closer. She was a good athlete, and I tried recruiting her for my soccer team (and failed miserably). But we always went to support her at her basketball and volleyball games.

Amy eventually graduated and went to Ms. Ameel's alma mater. In the following years, Amy had some serious ups and downs in her personal life, and she always seemed to lean on us for emotional support and advice. To be honest, she leaned more on Ms. Ameel, but since Ms. Ameel and I eventually got married (#winning), I wasn't left out of the loop.

The culmination of this long relationship with this wonderful young woman is a wonderful one, and joyous event. This past year, Amy and the love of her life got married, and Ms. Ameel was asked to officiate the ceremony. It's amazing that this young girl we met as an 8th grader so many years ago, would become like family, and we would be so honored as to be a part of the biggest day of her life.

While Amy had ups and downs in the years that we've known her (as all people do), it's been an honor and privilege to be a part of those years with her. As far as we're concerned, she's not 'like' family, she is family.

TRY THIS!

If you're in your first year of teaching, get ready to be blown away by some incredible your people. They'll melt your heart and warm your soul at times. But fast forward 10-15 years, and you might not remember some of the special, small moments you spent with your first class.

Try keeping a journal, where you only record positive moments with your students. It'll fill up fast, and 10 years from now, it will ring a tear to your eye when you dust it off and read it.

Last Word

I look back at these kids, and smile. I smile when I think of how strong Kris was, and how most young kids would have crumbled under the weight of what she dealt with. And yet, she flourished. I smile for the amazing professional Beth has become, and what an honor it was to be a part of her life. I smile at how honored I am to have made such an impact with Amy that still many years later, we consider each other family. I smile for the bright, yet far too short life of Tom, how he blossomed in his last years, and what a true honor it was to be a part of that. In the end, when I think back about any of my kids.... I smile.

Next Steps... And Thanks For Reading

This is where we sign off.... So stand up, stretch, get the blood flowing again. You've finished reading a book that will, hopefully, help you survive the toughest year of your new career. There was a lot in this book, so I hope you took notes. Whether you did or not, it'll be good to read applicable chapters over again, as the need arises through the next couple of school years, if not longer. After all, I'm finishing my second decade as a teacher, and even while writing this book, I realized just how much I needed to be reminded of these things.

So, what to do next?

To get things started, and to get the snowball slowly rolling down the snowy peak,

I'd suggest starting with the following two things:

1.   Start Small
2.   Get Support

By 'Start Small', I mean don't try incorporating 5 or 6 suggestions you found in this book, even if you are excited to do so. That much change all at once will only cause more stress, not alleviate it. Perhaps for the first few weeks, you focus just on separating the actions from the students, and not taking things so personally (heck, I'm still working on that one). Or maybe your focus is on writing quality, useful lesson plans, because that's something you've never done before. Each person reading this book has different strengths and different needs, and will have to make that choice on their own.

As far as 'Get Support', I simply ask that you don't try to redefine yourself as a teacher without help. Changing habits, in any aspect of one's life, is difficult. Think about how hard it is to change eating habits, or workout habits. People commonly use 'buddies' to help them with the process. Why would changing your mindset as a teacher be any less arduous? (Hint: It's not. It's more so).

Therefore, while I believe every chapter of this book is critical, I'd suggest making sure the 'Get Some Help Already' chapter is on the top of your priority list. With a seasoned veteran in your corner, every other change you look to make will be that much easier. As long as it's a veteran educator, it doesn't matter where you find them: down the hall, a friend at a different school, your district provided Instructional Coach, your Principal, or even a professional Instructional Coach like yours truly! I promise you, like the person who's starting a workout routine, the beginning of a great change is the hardest part, and it's when you'll need all the help you can get.

So, take a deep breath, use this book as a go-to guide often, reach out to people who will support you... and teach your heart out. The rest of us got your back.

References (*AKA Really Good Reading*)

1. Schoenbach, Ruth, et al. *Reading for Understanding*. Jossey-Bass, 2012.
2. Ullman, Ellen. "How To Plan Effective Lessons." *ASCD*, 2011, www.ascd.org .
3. Lorain, Peter. "Brain Development in Young Adolescents" NEA, 2018, www.nea.org
4. Burgess, Dave. *Teach Like A Pirate*. Dave Burgess Consulting, 2012.

About the Author

Dino is an educator of almost 20 years, at every level: K-12 as well as university. He's taught at schools in Michigan and California, been an Instructional Coach, taught as an adjunct professor at Fresno Pacific University and UC Merced, all with the goal of helping students and teachers be the best versions of themselves they can be, and supporting teachers to do the same with their students.

Dino is married to the most dedicated educator he's ever met, Margaret, who he lives with in Madera, CA. As much as they love living in California, a piece of their heart will always be in Detroit. It's a city of incredible people and culture, and was the city where Dino grew as an educator.

Dino's motivation for writing this book is simple: to help new teachers avoid the mistakes he made when he was new. While it's true that some things can only be learned through experience, it really makes no sense for each generation of teachers to repeat all the same mistakes over and over. So, hopefully this book can help new teachers avoid at least a few of the avoidable pitfalls.

Feel free to contact Dino with any of your questions or comments:

manganocoaching@gmail.com

Dino would like to dedicate this book to:

- ☐ Margaret, his partner in crime, and his inspiration.
- ☐ Rod, his spiritual compass... never in the history of the world has someone had a twin who's looked so little like them.
- ☐ Josh, who made sure he used the proper their/there/they're.
- ☐ Amanda, who is now beginning her own journey into the classroom. Get it, girl!
- ☐ Danielle, the best principal he's ever worked for.
- ☐ UPREP High School in Detroit, for being a home where he could become the teacher he wanted to be.
- ☐ Dino's fellow teachers up in the mountains... who would have thought he'd ever be teaching in a tiny town in the Sierra Nevada with such cool people.
- ☐ His parents. Every day he works with students who have truly rough home

lives. He's learned over the years how good he had it growing up.

☐ Every student who has allowed him to shape their life for the better. They are the reason he does what he does. They're the reason he gets up so early, drives so far, and pours his heart and soul into this calling.

www.ManganoCoaching.com

**TO SCHEDULE PERSONALIZED COACHING
WITH DINO,
IN PERSON OR ONLINE**

Made in the USA
Middletown, DE
13 June 2021